Kyoto in 3 Days – Travel Guide

This is a complete three days and two nights travel guide to Kyoto that will help you to explore the traditional and majestic city in 72 hours. It includes all tips, maps, information, and costs so you won't need to worry about spending time collecting information.

Our Kyoto travel guide provides a detailed itinerary that was developed by our travel experts team, which has travelled to Kyoto and personally tried all the suggested things. This carefully gathered information will let you feel like you have a personal travel guide, showing you around the city.

This travel guide to Kyoto is equally suitable for travellers who want to spend more time in the city. It focuses mostly on a medium budget. We can confirm that all made suggestions for attractions, restaurants, and accommodation are our own. Now grab a drink, relax and immerse yourself into reading about gorgeous Kyoto and what it can offer.

Contents

1st Day in Kyoto: Higashiyama/Gion, Downtown, and Fushimi Inari Shrine 63

2nd Day in Kyoto: Arashiyama Including Tenryu-ji, Bamboo Groove, Kinkaku-ji and Hot Springs 70

3rd Day in Kyoto: Northern Higashiyama and Leaving Kyoto 76

Introduction

Kyoto was, once, the capital of Japan, and its name can literally be translated as the 'Capital City.' The city of Kyoto is the capital of the Kyoto Prefecture which is in the Kansai region. Today, Kyoto is famous for being Japan's cultural capital as it has more than 1000 classical Buddhist temples, 400 unique Shinto temples, majestic Japanese gardens and imperial palaces, and traditional wooden houses. You will find 17 UNESCO World Heritage Sites in Kyoto (see the list of Unesco Sites here)

Kyoto is 458 kms (285 miles) away from Tokyo

Distances of Kyoto to Main Japanese Towns
Kyoto to Tokyo: 458km (285 miles)
Kyoto to Osaka: 55km (34 miles)
Kyoto to Sapporo: 1450km (901 miles)
Kyoto to Kobe: 75km (46 miles)
Kyoto to Hiroshima: 358km (223 miles)
Kyoto to Nagasaki: 781km (485 miles)

View of modern Kyoto buildings

When to Visit – The Weather

The best time to visit Kyoto is from March to May and from September to November.

 Summers are hot, humid and rainy, especially during June and July, and you should better avoid these months. September and October are usually hot, and the weather is like late spring weather, less rainy and not so humid. During November, the weather gets cooler and autumn foliage reaches its peak – a perfect time to visit Kyoto's temples and mountains. Traveling during winter is not recommended as it can get really cold.

Kyoto, Kyoto Prefecture, Japan

Overview   Graphs

Month	High / Low (°F)	Rain
January	48° / 33°	7 days
February	49° / 34°	8 days
March	56° / 38°	9 days
April	68° / 47°	9 days
May	76° / 57°	8 days
June	82° / 65°	11 days
July	89° / 73°	12 days
August	92° / 75°	8 days
September	84° / 68°	10 days
October	73° / 56°	7 days
November	63° / 45°	5 days
December	53° / 37°	5 days

Figure 2 Monthly Weather in Kyoto (F)

Kyoto, Kyoto Prefecture, Japan

Weather averages

Overview   Graphs

Month	High / Low (°C)	Rain
January	9° / 1°	7 days
February	10° / 1°	8 days
March	13° / 3°	9 days
April	20° / 9°	9 days
May	25° / 14°	8 days
June	28° / 19°	11 days
July	32° / 23°	12 days
August	33° / 24°	8 days
September	29° / 20°	10 days
October	23° / 13°	7 days
November	17° / 7°	5 days
December	11° / 3°	5 days

Figure 3 Monthly Weather in Kyoto (C)

Kyoto is surrounded by mountains that are just above 1000 meters above the sea level and has several rivers. As of 2015, Kyoto was ranked as the 9th largest city in Japan, and it covers an area of 827.83 square kilometers. There are only 1.5 million people living in Kyoto, which makes it one of the least populated cities in Japan.

The architecture of Kyoto can be described as traditional and religious due to the existence of many imperial palaces and temples. Even though Kyoto is a traditional city, you will also see many modern buildings and areas.

View of Kyoto's landscape and apartments

Kyoto is not only famous for its traditional buildings but also for the *geisha* (female entertainer/escort) and *kimono* (conventional Japanese clothes) culture. Most of Kyoto visitors and locals can be spotted wearing traditional garments while doing casual chores like grocery shopping, dining out or walking. Of course, it is entirely reasonable to not to wear traditional clothes.

Girls wearing traditional Geisha clothes in Kyoto

Kyoto is extremely popular among food lovers because of its tofu dishes, *kaiseki* (Japanese haute cuisine) cuisine, *shojin ryori* (Japanese Buddhist vegetarian dishes) and *Kyo-wagashi* (Kyoto sweets). Various types of restaurants serve not only Kyoto's specialties but also favorite Japanese dishes like soba, okonomiyaki, tempura, and sushi.
Even though Kyoto is considered a traditional and peaceful city, there are lots of high-end shops, fancy restaurants, and crazy nightclubs. Also, Kyoto is considered cheaper than Tokyo, so it's easier to enjoy the trip without counting money.

Night view of an alley in Kyoto

Transportation

Traveling to Kyoto

There are several different ways of reaching Kyoto from your home country. The most convenient and the quickest way to reach Kyoto is by plane. Of course, buses and trains are also convenient if you are already in Japan.

Kyoto doesn't have its own airport, and the closest airport is Osaka's Itami Airport that can be reached within an hour by bus from Kyoto's city center. To be more precise, the Osaka's Itami Airport is 52kms if you take the fast road with the tolls and you will need one hour and five minutes with a taxi or car, to reach the center of Kyoto.

Most of the flights are coming from Tokyo's Haneda Airport and only a few from Tokyo's Narita Airport. **Tip! Before flying to Kyoto, make sure that you are flying to Haneda and have enough time to transfer**. The flight takes about an hour, and regular fare is 23 000 yen ($208). However, you can get the book a combined ticket from your airlines or get discounted tickets for 9000 – 16 000 yen ($81 - $145).

From Inami Airport to Kyoto

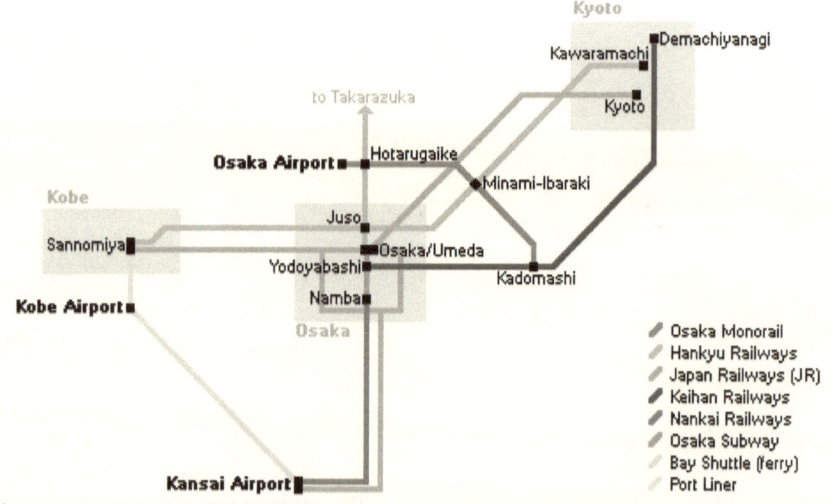

Transportation map of Inami Airport

- **Bus:** Every 20 minutes there is a direct bus from the airport to Kyoto. It takes about 1 hr 30 minutes to reach Kyoto and bus fare is 1310 yen ($12).
- **Monorail and train:** Monorail to Hotarugaike Station – takes about 2 minutes and costs 200 yen ($1.8). Transfer to the Hankyu Takarazuka Line and get off at Juso Station. Then transfer to the Hankyu Kyoto Line. The whole journey from Hotarugaike Station takes about 55 minutes and costs 470 yen ($4.27).
- **Monorail and Japan Railways (JR):** Monorail to Hotarugaike Station – takes about 2 minutes and costs 200 yen ($1.8). Transfer to the Hankyu Takarazuka Line and get off at Umeda Station (15-20 minutes, 220 yen ($2)). From Umeda station get into JR Kyoto Line to Kyoto. Takes about 30 minutes and costs 560 yen ($5).

From Tokyo to Kyoto

If you are already in Tokyo or purchased only a flight ticket to Tokyo, there are many different ways how to get to Kyoto from Japan's capital city. Look at the list and decide which way is the most convenient for you.

- **Shinkansen:** JR Tokaido Shinkansen connects Tokyo and Kyoto. Traveling time is from 140 minutes to 4 hours depending on the type of the train. Read more information about shinkansen trains here: http://bit.ly/2yNkczI. One way ticket price is about 13 500 yen ($122). If you are planning to travel more around Japan, consider buying a Japan Railway Pass: http://bit.ly/2KdfXmC.
- **Highway bus:** Highway bus is another option for traveling to Kyoto. It can take up to 7-8 hours. The price is from 3500 to 10 000 yen ($31-$90) one way depending on the bus type. Find out more about

highway bus types here: http://bit.ly/2IxWpnj. Also, consider purchasing a Japan Bus Pass that can reduce the price up to 3000 yen ($27) per trip. More information: http://bit.ly/2IxKyFM

- **Local trains:** Local trains are the trains that stop at every stop that exists. The trip to Kyoto from Tokyo can take up to 9 hours and can cost around 8210 yen ($74). However, you can get a Seishun 18 Kippu that can offer you a ticket for 2370 yen ($21). More information: http://bit.ly/2KiAWEE.

Traveling around Kyoto

Considering Kyoto's size, it has a straightforward but not very well-developed transportation system around the city. It has two subway lines, a bus network and several railways lines that aren't always conveniently connected with each other. Sometimes it can be easier to take a taxi or hire a bicycle for your whole stay.

We highly recommend you get an IC Card if you are planning on using public transportation. IC Card lets you pay for buses and subways around Japan. It is more convenient to carry this card around instead of using your credit card. For the Kyoto transportation, you need to purchase an Icoca or Pitapa card those are Kansai region's IC Cards. It will cost around 1500 yen ($13). More about IC Cards you can find on this website: http://bit.ly/2IyDw3p.

You can also purchase a Kansai One Pass that is a particular IC Card that was created especially for foreigners. It works exactly the same as others IC Cards and gives you discounts at various attractions around the Kansai region. If you aren't planning buying an IC Card, we recommend purchasing at least a one-day transportation cards such as Kyoto Subway One Day Card (600 yen ($5.44)) or Kyoto One Day Bus Card (600 yen ($5.44)). Please, remember that subway one day card can't be used on buses, and bus one day card can't be used on subways.

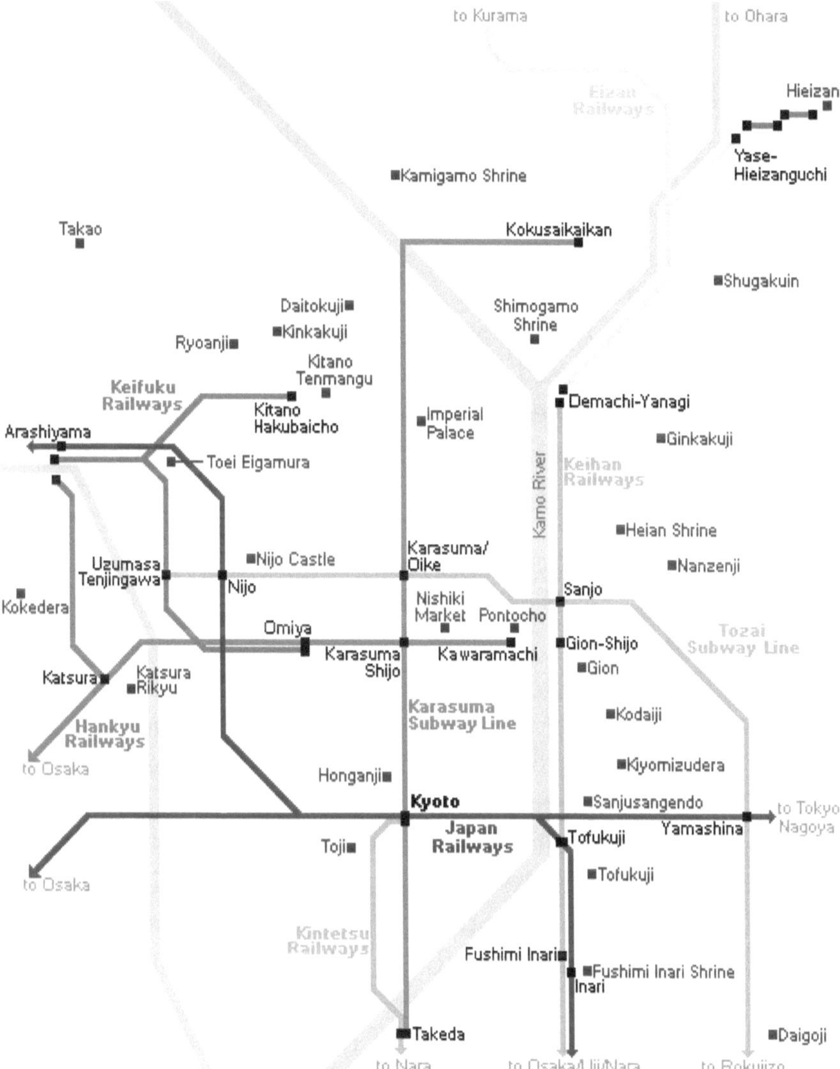

Map of Kyoto's subway and railway lines

- **Subway:** There are two subway lines in Kyoto: Karasuma Line (runs from south to north) and Tozai Line (runs from east to west).
- **Japan Railways (JR):**

a.) Tokaido Shinkansen – perfect for visiting southern Kyoto's attractions like Fushimi Inari temple.

b.) Hankyu Railway – connects Kyoto with Osaka. Perfect for traveling around western Kyoto towards Osaka.

c.) Keifuku Railway – operates two trams like trains in north-western Kyoto. The ride itself can be seen as an attraction as it's old and unusual train. Get this train if you want to visit Kinkakuji temple.

d.) Keihan Railway – runs along the river and can be used to access southern Kyoto. This line isn't connected to Kyoto Station.

e.) Eizan Railway – has to lines that are going through northern Kyoto.

f.) Kintetsu Railway – connects Kyoto with Nara.

- **Taxi:** Kyoto has a high concentration of taxis that are usually used for traveling short distances. The basic rate for the first 2 kilometers is 650 yen ($5.90) and 80 yen ($0.72) for every additional kilometer.

- **Bicycle:** The easiest way to get around Kyoto is to rent a bike from any of Kyoto's rental shops. The rental price is 1000-1500 yen ($9-$13) per day. It is the easiest way to get around Kyoto, especially during the rush hours.

- **Bus:** Kyoto has a quite good bus system that serves significant tourist sights. Green City Bus is for central areas and has the most services, Red Kyoto Bus serves some out of city attractions. The ride rate is 230 yen ($2) per ride. **Tip! Always ride a bus from the closest subway station to the destination as the traffic in Kyoto is terrible and coaches often get too crowded.** More information about buses: http://bit.ly/2tGoukn

- **Uber:** There is Uber in Kyoto but it's more expensive and will serve you worse than the regular taxis, so don't bother with it.

Back view of Keifuku train

Useful Travel Information

Official Kyoto Travel Website: https://kyoto.travel/en
Official Language: Japanese
Sizes: Metric System (kilograms, centimetres, C)
Money: Japan currency is yen, money can be exchange at 'Authorized Foreign Exchange Bank' – written in English. 1000 Yens are 9 USD. The Yen is subdivided into 100 Sens. Coins come in denominations of 500, 100, 50, 10, 5 and 1 yen.
ATMs: You can withdraw money from any ATM (CityBank doesn't charge you). However, there are no ATMs that are open for 24/7. You have to withdraw cash before 5 PM.
Cash: You can use credit/debit cards to pay at big shops. However, Japan is a cash-based society, so you must have some cash on hand. Visa, Mastercard, Maestro and JCB are the most widely accepted. American Express and Diners are not that common. The large establishments (large businesses and hotels) are easily accepting credit cards. The smaller establishments often ask for cash.
Tipping: Japan doesn't have a tipping system. Also, lots of restaurants/hotels include tips in the receipt. Tipping is not expected in Japan and no one asks for tips. Sometimes, it may even be considered as rude and you may offend people by giving them a tip.
GMT: GMT +9
Wifi: Free wi-fi is available on bus or subway stations, convenience store, some tourists' attractions and shopping centers.
Internet Speed: The average speed is 17.4Mbps, which is even faster than what you will meet in US. Wi-Fi coverage is high and you will find wi-fi in many cafes, bars, hotels and restaurants.
Sockets and Plugs: Japan doesn't use three-pronged plugs so you will need an adaptor.
Japan uses 100V, 50/60Hz, with sockets and plugs Type A and B.

Type A

Type B

Dial Code: +81 (81 is the country code for Japan)
Driving License: You will need an International Driving Permit (IDP) together with your original driving license. You can get an IDP at your local automobile association at your home country.
Driving Side: In Japan, cars drive on the left side. Most cars have an automatic transmission.
Emergency Numbers: Police 110, Ambulance 119, Fire Department 119

Where to Stay in Kyoto

Kyoto is a traditional yet modern city which offers various areas to stay. The city is divided into districts that provide different kinds of attractions such as nightlife, high-end restaurants or a peaceful nature. Below you will find our detailed guide of Kyoto's areas and best hotels, guesthouses, and Ryokan (traditional Japanese inn). Since Kyoto is quite compacted, all our picked places to stay are convenient for the sightseeing, transport, nightlife, and shopping, and, of course, we have considered three different budgets (luxury, mid-range and budget travel) while making our guide. Also, we have selected the most popular districts that will let you experience Kyoto to the fullest.
See below the map of the most popular districts in Kyoto.

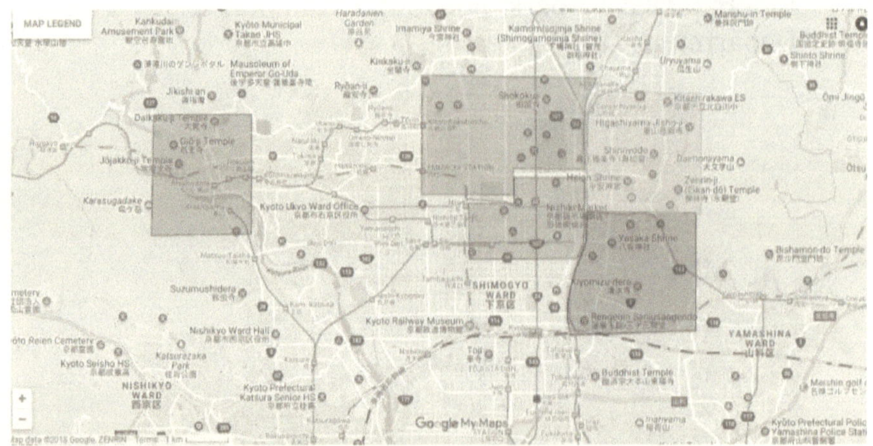

Get the full map here: *http://bit.ly/2z73hsn*

Map Legend:
Grey – Arashiyama
Pink – Central Kyoto
Green – Downtown Kyoto
Orange – Northern Higashiyama
Purple – Southern Higashiyama

Arashiyama

Arashiyama is considered as one of the best Kyoto's areas to go sightseeing. It is located on the foot of Kyoto's western mountains. This area is perfect for a relaxing stay between hills and majestic mountains. The main Arashiyama's attractions are Tenryu-Ji temple and bamboo forest.

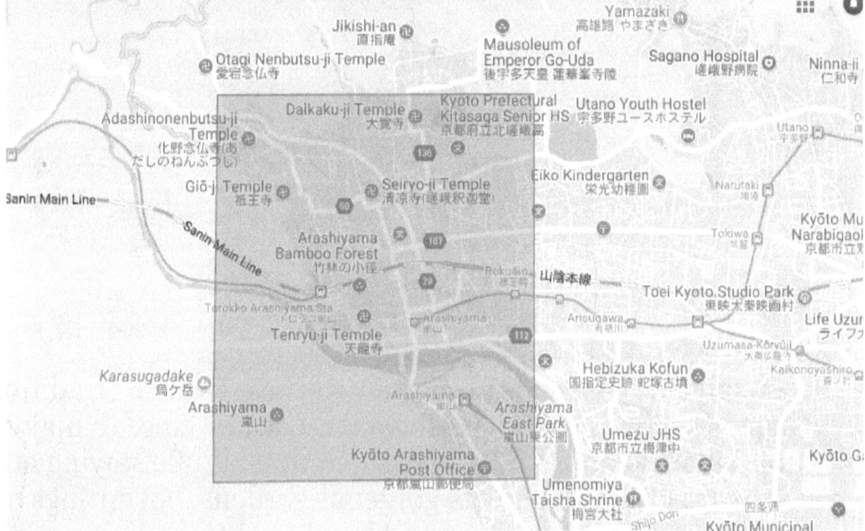

Even though it looks like a perfect place to stay, however, Arashiyama is quite far from the central Kyoto – about 30 minutes' drive. Also, since it's a popular area for the tourists, the main street, and specific sights can be really crowded from early morning to late evening.

Best Places to Stay in Arashiyama

#Arashiyama Benkei: https://booki.ng/2Mzwluc

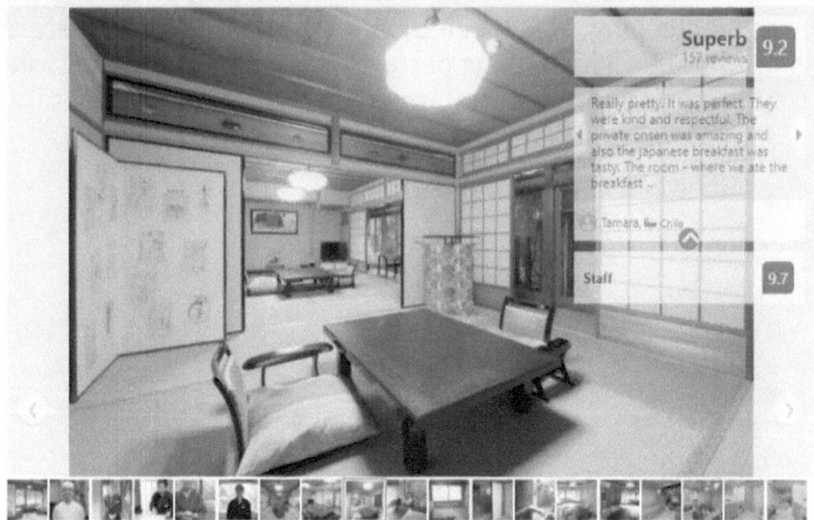

Arashiyama Benkei is absolutely the best Ryokan (traditional Japanese inn) around Arashiyama. Located close to major tourist attractions and great restaurants. While staying at this Ryokan, you can enjoy its gorgeous gardens, hot springs and traditional Kyoto's dinner and breakfast. All bedrooms are designed as traditional Japanese room so you will experience what's like to stay at a traditional Japanese house. This is a luxury stay, so be prepared to pay around $600 per night for a double room with shared bathroom without breakfast fee. Breakfast at the inn is $23.

Japaning Hotel Liv Ranrokaku

https://booki.ng/2MDWV5B

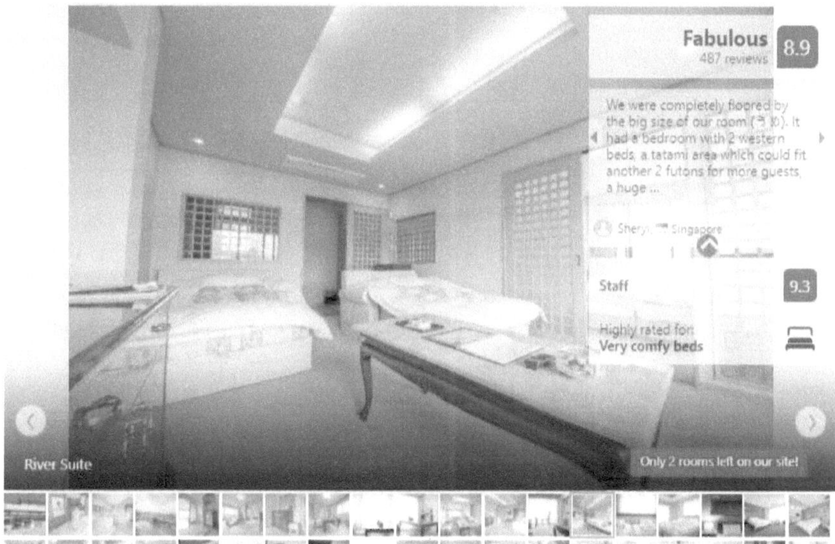

This hotel is still considered to be a Ryokan but more modern than the previously mentioned one. Japaning Hotel has perfect spacious rooms and outdoor hot springs with a great view of Kyoto. Hotel is hidden away from busy Arashiyama streets, just next by the river. Monkey park and bamboo forest are the closest tourist attractions near the hotel. This is a mid-range hotel and a double room costs around $128 per night. However, be aware that don't typically serve food so you would need to find places to eat close by.

We highly recommend this hotel as it has excellent price deals for single and double rooms, all rooms are spacious and well equipped. Most likely that you won't find any better deal around Arashiyama.

Guest house Murasaki is a perfect place for a budget travelers as the night rate per double room with shared bathroom starts from $26. The guest house is located near popular tourist attractions such as Manga Museum and hot springs. You won't find a better budget guesthouse in Arashiyama than Murasaki.

Central Kyoto

Central Kyoto is probably one of the largest districts in Kyoto. This district can be described as an old yet modern district. There are numerous amount of contemporary office buildings, convenience stores, supermarkets and shopping streets. However, you can find a gorgeous Imperial Gardens, the famous Nijo Castle, and some small traditional Japanese gardens.

Central Kyoto is a great place to stay if you like going out or shopping after a long day of sightseeing. Some large high-end shops and restaurants offer foreign food. Also, central Kyoto is suitable for transportation as there are quite a few subway stations and bus stops all over the district. The district is quite flat, so it will be easier to walk or cycle.

The only one downside of central Kyoto is that all major tourist attractions apart from Nijo Castle and Imperial

Gardens are quite far, so you would need to use public transportation to visit all the places instead of walking.

Central Kyoto's accommodation is usually in a mid-price range so you can find excellent hotels for an affordable price. Take a look at our recommendations below.

Best Places to Stay in Central Kyoto
#Noku Kyoto https://booki.ng/2KqsKlI

Noku Kyoto is a majestic boutique hotel that is located close to Marutamachi subway station and next to Imperial Park. Also, it is very easily reachable from JR Kyoto Station – only 7-minute ride on Karasuma line. The rooms are very spacious, well equipped with fridge and flat screen TV, and free wifi. The main attractions of Central Kyoto district can be reached on foot (about 10-minute walk). Double king room rate is $166 per night.

#ANA Crowne Plaza Hotel Kyoto
https://booki.ng/2tVcNc5

This nice elegant mid-range hotel is located near Nijo Castle (just 1-minute walk). Crowne Plaza Hotel Kyoto is a western type hotel that offers excellent large modern rooms and a breakfast buffet that is included in the room rate.
Expensive rooms include free snacks and drinks. Also, you can find various excellent restaurants in the hotel where you can enjoy a few drinks and cuisine from different countries. There are outdoor and indoor pool with saunas that you can enjoy for an extra cost or get a deal with everything included. Crowne Plaza Hotel provides free shuttle buses to Kyoto station, those buses run every 15 minutes. However, you can always take a subway as the hotel is close to the Nijojo-Mae subway station. The double room cheapest rate is from $126 to $166.

#Grids Kyoto Shijo Kawaramachi Hotel&Hostel

https://booki.ng/2z1f6QL

This hostel is perfect for the travelers who are traveling on a budget. Lots of main Kyoto's attractions can be reached on foot and with public transport if you want to save some time.

The hostel offers simple breakfast for $5.25. A double room costs $55 per night and bunk bed in 12-bed dorm costs around $15.7 per night. You can select if you want mixed or single gender dorm room.

Downtown Kyoto

Downtown Kyoto is connected to the Central Kyoto district and is the oldest part of Kyoto. Downtown covers an area on the west bank of Kamo River. The district includes historically famous Pontocho Geisha area and a modern shopping street Shijo.

Downtown Kyoto is the most famous district to stay while visiting the city. It is perfect for sightseeing (especially temples), shopping, eating out, nightlife and fantastic street food markets.

You can reach southern Higashiyama on foot and use any of the two city's subway lines. Don't be surprised by seeing narrow allow, vibrant colors and lots of street vendors.

Best Places to Stay in Downtown Kyoto

#The Ritz-Carlton Kyoto https://booki.ng/2zdvP3t

The Ritz Carlton Hotel can be described as modern yet traditional, luxurious yet modest and expensive but worth the price. This hotel is perfect for couples who would like to enjoy luxurious Kyoto as the hotel has an ideal location, restaurant, bar and magnificent views overlooking the river and rear garden.

The cheapest room rate is $1393 per night for two people; for one person is $1281. However, it is possible to get some deals at a lower price.

#Solaria Nishitetsu Hotel Kyoto Premier
https://booki.ng/2lO3kj2

Hotel is highly recommended for the location as it overlooks the Kamo River. Lots of temples and famous places to go out are easily reachable on foot and by public transportation. Rooms are spacious and modern, well equipped with bottled water, toothbrushes and toiletries. There is an indoor hot spring that can be enjoyed with an extra charge. Double room rate is $152 for two people without breakfast or $200 for two people with breakfast buffet.

Hotel Gracery Kyoto Sanjo is a perfect budget hotel that is very conveniently located for the various railway and subway lines. Rooms are huge and modern, and hardly any noise can be heard from the streets. Shijo shopping district is just minutes away, so you can easily spend your night shopping. Double room rate per night is $91 for two people and $89 for a one person. You can purchase breakfast for $18 per person.

Northern Higashiyama

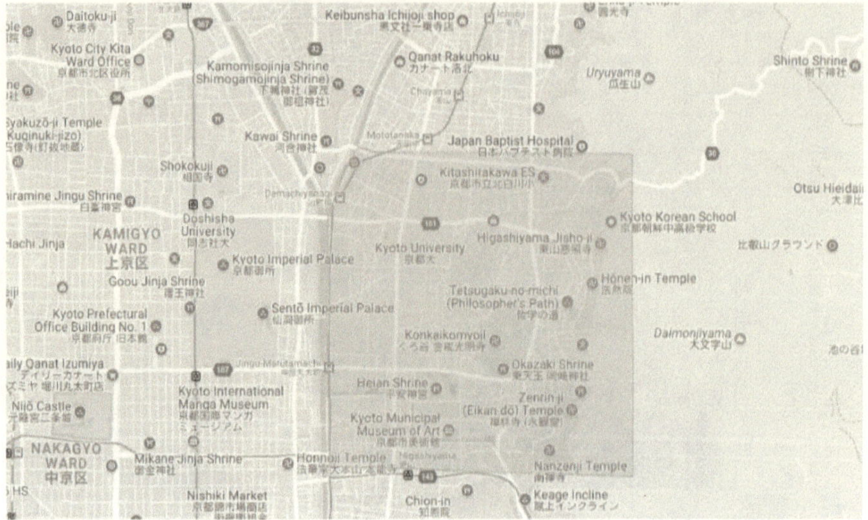

Northern Higashiyama is filled with majestic ancient temples, shrines and Japanese Zen gardens and is connected to Southern Higashiyama. The most famous attraction is the Path of Philosophy – a walking route from Ginkaku-Ji Temple (The Silver Pavilion) to Nanzen-Ji Temple. Northern Higashiyama has a limited choice of nightlife, shops, and restaurants, so there is a significant possibility that you will have to travel to the Central Kyoto or Downtown Kyoto for shopping.

To be added, Northern Higashiyama is a perfect neighborhood for travelers who like a peaceful atmosphere and less crowded streets. This district can offer quietness as there are not many hotels, hostels or guesthouses (not many places to stay in at all), however, it is full of *Ryokans* (traditional Japanese inns). *Ryokans* can be a pretty expensive option to stay in. However, it's a great experience, and you can find our recommended *Ryokans* below.

Best Places to Stay in Northern Higashiyama
#Ryokan Inn Yoshida-sanso https://booki.ng/2lN2Qtv

This *Ryokan* was once a royal residence and is a perfect place to experience traditional Japanese stay. Located on the foot of beautiful mountains and has excellent views of traditional Japanese gardens. All rooms are traditional Japanese rooms equipped with futon mats and have a shared bathroom. A double room costs $558 per night with breakfast.

#Kyoto Garden Ryokan Yachiyo
https://booki.ng/2KpvIqy

This comfortable *Ryokan* is located next to the famous Nanzen-Ji Temple and is surrounded by beautiful Japanese gardens. It has 20 well-equipped rooms, and some of the rooms have an open-air wooden bath.

There are standard twin rooms and studio rooms that has a similar rate per night. The usual price per night for a double room is $198. However, you can get a sweet deal with breakfast included in the price.

#Kyoto style small inn Iru https://booki.ng/2tSRFmK

It is a small guest house that offers Japanese style rooms for an affordable price. Kyoto Style Small Inn Iru also provides bicycle rental so you can explore unique paths of Kyoto. Around this guest house, there are a few restaurants and bars that offer great local food and is very convenient for the public transportation.

Twin room rate per night is $61 with breakfast included. If you are on a tight budget, this guest house is just for you.

Southern Higashiyama – Gion

Gion is closely connected to Southern Higashiyama (mostly Southern Higashiyama is referred to as Gion) and is the most famous and oldest Geisha district where you get a glimpse into the past of Japan. You will be able to see lots of girls dressed as Geishas and entertaining visitors. Also, the architecture makes you feel like you stepped into medieval Kyoto.

More in the mountains lies Southern Higashiyama with its colorful temples, shrines, various parks, and Zen gardens. This district is crowded all the time as it has the most famous traditional tea houses, restaurants, and ancient temples. Despite being crowded, Southern Higashiyama/Gion is the perfect place to stay during your visit as there are so many great places to stay in and all major tourist attractions are located close by. By staying in Southern Higashiyama, you are getting the best that Kyoto can offer.

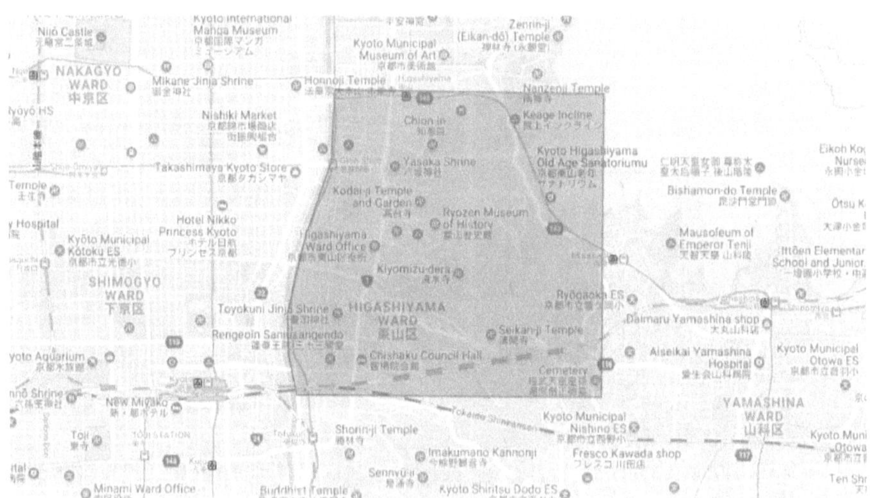

Best Places to Stay in Southern Higashiyama/Gion

 # Gion Hatanaka https://booki.ng/2KwtKVq

Gion Hatanaka is very luxurious stay close by famous historical Gion district and is incredibly popular between tourists and Japanese visitors. Gion Hatanaka is a modern *Ryokan* that will make your first stay in a *Ryokan* be an enjoyable experience.

Rooms are spacious, amazing traditional Japanese décor, comfortable seating area and a great balcony with stunning views. All rooms have a private bathroom that has a traditional Japanese soaking tub – wooden bath.

Gion Hatanaka is close by subway and bus stations. Also, there are lots of temples that are easily reachable on foot. Also, you can easily rent a bike or use one of the walking tours that *Ryokan* is offering for its guests.

Room for two people costs $547 per night. For this price two people can stay in a triple room and enjoy great grand breakfast and dinner – meals are included in the price.

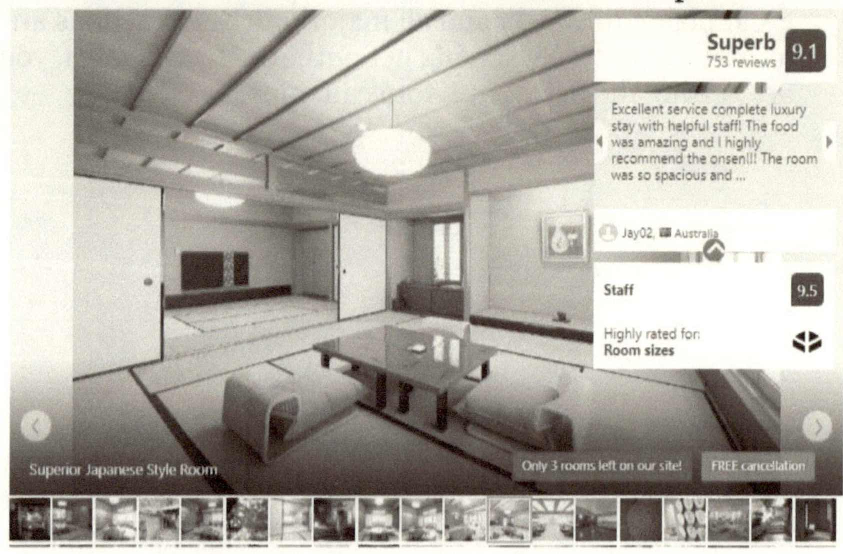

#Hana-Touro Hotel Gion https://booki.ng/2tYEr84

Modern and boutique hotel located just a block away from the heart of Gion. This modern yet traditional hotel offers excellent large rooms that are equipped with flat screen TV and comfortable beds.

There is a great restaurant, a perfect rooftop lounge that offers majestic views of Kyoto's temples. Also, you can find a bike hire if you want to explore Kyoto by bike.

Standard double room's rate is $199 for two people per night.

#Laon Inn Gion Shinmonzen

https://booki.ng/2MIWOpe

This hotel can be described as a holiday flat rental that has shared the reception and lounge area. Rooms are very spacious, has all the necessary things for your stay such as wifi, TV, kitchenette, air con, and washing machine.

It is very close to the main street, Gion, various temples and public transport stops. Standard room rate for two people per night is $56 that is a really value-for-money price for the Southern Higashiyama district.

We hope that our guide to Kyoto's district helped you to decide where you want to stay during your trip to Kyoto. We highly recommend any of the previously mentioned places. However, we have decided to choose **Kyoto Garden Ryokan Yachiyo** (Northern Higashiyama) for our three days itinerary as it offers a great traditional Japanese stay and is located close to major tourist attractions.

Frequently Asked Questions about Staying in Kyoto

1.) Which area is the best if I am traveling on a budget?

We recommend you to stick with Central Kyoto, Downtown Kyoto or even Kyoto Station area as there are a lot of hostels and guesthouses that usually charge less than $50 per night. Also, fewer visitors stay around those areas so you can quickly get a room. However, consider the fact that not all hostels or guesthouses are going to be modern, comfortable and quiet.

2.) How cheap is Kyoto's accommodation?

Comparing with Tokyo room rates, Kyoto is quite cheap as you can get a quite large room for the same price as the smallest sleeping space in Tokyo. Everything that comes below $100 you should consider as being cheap.

3.) Is it safe to rent an Airbnb?

Airbnb is a safe option to stay in Kyoto. However, there aren't many available options and some of the apartments' rate per night is higher than a great room in a luxurious Kyoto's hotel. If you are traveling with a group, then I would recommend renting an Airbnb.

4.) Where to stay if I want to see the most of Kyoto?

We recommend staying in Northern or Southern Higashiyama/Gion as these areas have magnificent temples, old alleys and fantastic tea houses and restaurants. Also, it has excellent public transport connections, and it's easy to reach other major tourist sights. Also, Downtown Kyoto is good for the major tourist attractions and has excellent transportation to reach further sights in Arashiyama.

5.) Would you recommend to include breakfast in the room rate?

If there is a possibility, yes. Breakfast can cost from $10 to $30 depending on your accommodation. It's a little bit overpriced if you don't eat a big breakfast. However, we highly recommend eating lunch-like breakfast at your accommodation to save your time in the morning, and you will have more time sightseeing.

6.) Should I stay at a traditional Japanese inn (*Ryokan*) or at western style accommodation?

As you are visiting Kyoto, we highly recommend staying at *Ryokan* to experience the Japanese culture. Most of Ryokans are very minimalistic and can be rather expensive. However, it's a very peaceful and unforgettable experience.

7.) Do you recommend doing a 'Couchsurfing'?

Kyoto is a safe city. However, all towns have strange people who want to benefit from you. We would recommend you not to risk your own safety and stay in a legit place instead of searching for free accommodation.

Fun Things to Do in Kyoto

Kyoto is a traditional city that has lots of fun activities for all travelers and locals. It is impossible to name all the possible activities that you can do during your visit. Due to this reason, we have made a perfect list of the best and the most memorable activities you could do. So don't worry, there is plenty of choices.

Hiking Tour of Mt. Takao

Shrine at Mt. Takao

Mountain Takao is a mountainous area in the north of Kyoto
– takes about 1 hour by bus to reach the mountain. Takao has
3 beautiful ancient temples: Kozanji, Jingoji, and Saimyoji.
The hiking trails are accessible, suitable for amateurs and
families. The most famous trail passes through Kozanji
temple and leads to the top passing through beautiful flowers
and high trees. It is a 6 hours and about 8 kilometers day
hike.
If you are interested in this tour with a guide, visit the
website below to get all the details: http://bit.ly/2lT536M.

Kyoto Zen Garden Tour

Japan is famous for its Zen gardens, especially Kyoto as it has
the most famous Zen garden in Japan – Nanzenji Temple
Zen Monastery that was started in 1611. It's not highly visited
by tourists, so the atmosphere is very peaceful, and you are
able to look at everything without any queues. Also, while
visiting the garden, you can visit the temple at the same time.
The tour is about 3 hours 30 minutes long and is led by
American landscape designer who will be able to answer all
your questions, talk about garden's secret history and tell all
essential facts about compositions in the garden.
If you are fascinated to visit a hidden Kyoto's treasure, take a
look at this site for more information: http://bit.ly/2KzkTSU.

Zen Garden at Nanzenji Temple

Night-time Old Kyoto Tour with Food

Geiko entering into one of the restaurants in Gion District

Tour starts at Gion district that is well-known for being the oldest district in Kyoto filled with narrow alleys, streets, evening entertainment and modern-day Geiko (Geisha). This tour specializes in Kyoto's history facts that you won't be able to know from simple temple visits such as why Kyoto call Geisha as Geiko and much more!

The tour involves tasting some local traditional food and beer (or stronger drinks depending on your taste). After eating and drinks, a local guide will lead you through dark old alleys where you will be able to see how Kyoto's locals treasure their tradition. And the last part of the tour involves more food and more drinks! Prices and more information can be found here: http://bit.ly/2IQIuc0.

Kyoto Tea House Tour with *Maiko*

Maiko – an apprentice Geisha (Geiko in Kyoto)

Kyoto is very well-known for its *Geiko (Geisha)* and *Maiko* (apprentice *Geisha*) culture as it's still alive in the modern Kyoto. This tour offers you an opportunity to get into ochaya tea house that is not usually open to the public. The trip will last for 2 hours, and you will be able to enjoy a company of *Maiko* who will serve you drinks, play easy games with you, chat with you via interpreter-guide and show her dancing skills. It's a great experience for guys and girls as you will be able to see an authentic Japanese *Maiko*.

More information about the tour is here: http://bit.ly/2lRwkXf.

Arashiyama Rickshaw Tour

Arashiyama is a rural Kyoto's district that is filled with quiet streets, ancient temples and nature everywhere. One of the most famous ways to explore Arashiyama areas is to hire a rickshaw and enjoy a peaceful day. This tour offers you about 3 hours of excellent rickshaw ride through various temples, parks, and other areas. Several tour options lead to different paths so you can personalize your rickshaw tour depending on what you would like to see.

More details about the tour, its options and guide can be found here: http://bit.ly/2Nta7eu.

Empty rickshaw in the street

Spiritual Kyoto: A Detailed Guide of Shrines and Temples

Kyoto has the highest concentration of Buddhist temples and Shinto shrines so the city itself is very spiritual and locals tend to visit temples or shrines a lot. Locals go to pray, relax their mind or enjoy the breath-taking scenery.

Kyoto has literally more than hundreds of temples and shrines that are very similar to foreigner's eyes. However, these sacred buildings have different purposes and can be distinguished easily if you know more about them. Below you will find the main differences between the shrine and temple. Shinto shrines usually have a '*torii*' gate at the entrance and a purification fountain which provides fresh water. You are welcomed to wash your hands or drink, however, make sure that the ladle isn't touching your mouth directly. You will see people bowing and praying, but as a foreigner, you aren't obligated to do the same. While visiting these sacred places, you must follow the rules for visitors such as don't smoke, be quiet, don't take photos where is not allowed and etc.

Torri Gate in front of the shrine

You can recognize Buddhist temples by a '*sanmon*' gate that is standing by the entrance. At the gate, you can show your respect and give a short prayer. Unlike in other Southeast

Asian countries, Japanese temples are mostly used to store and display sacred objects, and only Buddhists pray at the temples. Rules are very similar to shrine rules so you will need to pay attention to the signage around the temple.

Main sanmon gate marking the entrance to Nanzen-Ji temple

As temples and shrines are the most important and famous Kyoto's attractions, we have made this guide to introduce some of the most famous sacred ancient buildings around Kyoto. This detailed guide will help you to navigate between Kyoto's areas with beautiful temples and shrines. We can make you assure that some of the temples and shrines are going to be included in our three-day itinerary. However, you are welcomed to visit more of those buildings during your free time or make some alterations depending on your needs.

UNESCO World Heritage

Kyoto has sixteen temples and shrines included in UNESCO World Heritage list. All of those sites are easily accessible from Kyoto. Below you will find all sixteen places and some information about them.

Temples

Nishi Hongwan-Ji

This temple represents the Momoyama period (1573-1603) and was built with the purpose to impress. Temple has large buildings, gold altars and various items that are included in the National Treasures list. Nishi Hongwan-Ji practices Shin Buddhism. More information about the temple's history: https://kyoto.travel/en/shrine_temple/122.

To-Ji

To-Ji temple is famous for its 5-story pagoda that is as high as 55 meters. The temple was built in 796, and its architecture is a mix of traditional Chinese, Indian and Japanese architectural styles. More information: https://kyoto.travel/en/shrine_temple/123.

To-Ji temple and its 5-story pagoda

Byodo-in

This temple once was a famous villa that was converted into a temple in 1052, and only one building is the original one – Phoenix Hall (Amida-do). Temple has a beautiful pond and an impressive golden Amida Buddha. There are lots of souvenir shops and great tea houses around the temple. More information: https://kyoto.travel/en/shrine_temple/124.

Kozan-ji

Kozan-Ji is a mountain forest temple that was built in the 13th century. Temple is a very tranquil and remote place to enjoy the nature. Temple has various Buddhism art treasures that are worth seeing. More information can be found here: https://kyoto.travel/en/shrine_temple/125.

Mt. Hiei-zan Enryaku-Ji

This temple is basically a monastery complex at the top of the mountain and is considered to be one of the primary spiritual centers of Japanese culture. Since this temple complex is so old and important, there are numerous legends about the temple buildings and items. The most famous legend is that in the Central Hall there are lanterns that have remained alight for more than 1200 years. Unlike other temples, this one was substantially involved in politics and even had its own army. This temple practices Tendai Buddhism and you can find more information at this site: https://kyoto.travel/en/shrine_temple/126.

Saiho-Ji

Saiho-Ji or Koke-Dera temple's main attraction is the natural moss garden. Because of numerous visitors, the temple has a restricted admission system: you need to make a reservation in advance if you want to visit the garden. You can always ask your hotel administrator to arrange a booking for you. More information can be found here: https://kyoto.travel/en/shrine_temple/127.

Daigo-Ji

Daigo-ji temple is located in the mountain Daigo and is widely known as 'Temple of Flowers.' It has a few main huge buildings, some small buildings, and a 5-story pagoda. If you would like to know more about the temple, click here: https://kyoto.travel/en/shrine_temple/129.

Ginkaku-Ji (Jisho-Ji)

Jisho-Ji temple mostly known as Ginkaku-Ji temple or Temple of the Silver Pavilion. Temple belongs to Buddhist Shokoku School that practices Rinzai Zen. It's an exquisite temple that is resting on the foot of Kyoto's eastern mountains. It has a sister temple – Kinkaku-Ji or The Golden Pavilion that is also located in Kyoto. Read more about the temple's history here: https://kyoto.travel/en/shrine_temple/130.

Kiyomizu-Dera

Kiyomizu-Dera is probably the most famous temple in Kyoto as it has a massive main wooden building with various crafts that make it look grander. Various romantic legends surround Kiyomizu-dera's history that is supposed to be inappropriate for the sacred place. Some of the buildings are designed as national treasures, and there is a shrine inside the temple complex buildings. Read the more extended introduction to Kiyomizu-Dera temple here: https://kyoto.travel/en/shrine_temple/131.

Side view of Kiyomizu-dera main building

Ninna-Ji

This temple is probably not very widely known between tourists, but it has everything from ponds to ancient stones in

the garden. Very popular for its cherry blossoms and impressive landscape. You can find more information and history facts here:
https://kyoto.travel/en/shrine_temple/133.

Ryoan-Ji

Ryoan-Ji is a Zen temple that is famous for its rock garden that makes all visitors curious about the garden's layout. Even though the temple was built in 1450, no one knows how the rock garden was formed and who created it. Temple has nice traditional buildings complex and great trails to walk around. More information such as admission fee and opening times you can find here:
https://kyoto.travel/en/shrine_temple/134.

Kinkaku-Ji

Kinkaku-Ji temple or The Golden Pavilion is located in a big pond and is a number one place that is must-see in Kyoto. The strangest thing about Kinkaku-Ji temple is that it's not used for prays and doesn't practice any kind of Buddhism. You can consider Kinkaku-Ji temple as a museum or storehouse for the sacred relics. More information about its history is here: https://kyoto.travel/en/shrine_temple/132.

Kinkaku-Ji Golden Pavilion

Tenryu-Ji

This temple was built in 1339 and is a temple of Rinzai School. It has a large Zen garden that features huge maple trees and a pond making it a perfect place to relax and gather all your thoughts. Temple is usually quiet as there aren't many visitors walking around, however during autumn temple welcomes thousands of visitors as everyone wants to take a look at beautifully colored maple trees. If you are interested in visiting the temple, find more information here: https://kyoto.travel/en/shrine_temple/135.

Shrines

Shimogamo-Jinja

Known as Kamomioja-jinja and is a family shrine of Kamo clan that inhabited the area of Kyoto. This shrine is resting between two rivers and in the middle of a thick forest. Shimogamo-Jinja is a sister shrine of Kamigamo-Jinja, and they both host an Aoi Matsuri festival – a parade of people wearing period costumes. More information can be found here: https://kyoto.travel/en/shrine_temple/120.

Kamigamo-jinja

Is the oldest shrine in Kyoto, dating back to the 7th century before Kyoto was established. This shrine is dedicated to harvesting deity Wakeikazuchi that is also the guardian of Kyoto. More information about the shrine's history you can found here: https://kyoto.travel/en/shrine_temple/121

Ujigami-jinja

This shrine is located in a tranquil place near the Ujigawa River and Byodo-in temple. Shrine was built for an Imperial Prince who committed suicide to solve a dispute over the throne. It is a very simple shrine, but gorgeous. If you would like to find out more information, visit this website: https://kyoto.travel/en/shrine_temple/128.

Hall of Ujigami-Jinja shrine

Map of UNESCO World Heritage Temples and Shrines

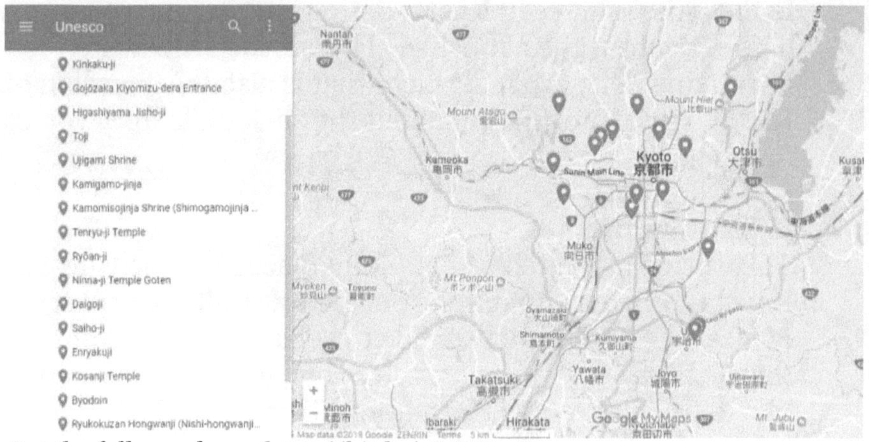

Get the full map here: http://bit.ly/2MQRmR7

North Kyoto Temples and Shrines

North Kyoto area has the oldest temples and shrines in all of Japan. Most of temples and shrines are in the mountains that are very easily accessible and cool during the hot summer.

Temples

Daisen-in

This temple features a Zen architecture that looks very aesthetic and modest. While visiting this temple, it is recommended to take a closer look at its garden as it is considered one of the most elegant gardens in Japan. Information: https://kyoto.travel/en/shrine_temple/137.

Daitoku-ji

This temple is an excellent example of Japanese Zen Buddhism and has several sub temples that are functioning on their own. Daitoku-ji can be referred to as a small temple village. Find out about temple's history here: https://kyoto.travel/en/shrine_temple/138.

Daitoku-ji temple and its garden

Genko-an

Temple belongs to the Soto sect of Zen Buddhism. It famous for its historical Buddha and Kannon Bodhisattva statues, and 'bloody ceiling' – the ceiling was made from Fushimi castle floorboards where very loyal soldiers killed themselves to protect their lord. There are some fascinating legends about these floorboards that monks will happily tell you. More information: https://kyoto.travel/en/shrine_temple/139.

Kurama-dera

Temple was founded in 770 and has its own sect and practices of Buddhism where mountain spirits play the most significant part in worship. It is entirely located in the mountains so you might have trouble as you will need to hike all the way up to the unfriendly peak. Information: https://kyoto.travel/en/shrine_temple/143.

Manshu-in

Basically is a garden with a little temple. Manshu-in temple represents Shoin architecture style that was popular during the Edo period. It has many paintings by artists of Kano school. More about its history: https://kyoto.travel/en/shrine_temple/144.

Shisen-do

This temple was built in 1641 as a mountain hermitage. Temple features lots of ancient Chinese poets, and its name can be translated as 'Hall of Immortal Poets.' More about its architecture: https://kyoto.travel/en/shrine_temple/146.

Shoden-ji

This temple uses the same floorboards as Genko-an. It is a tranquil place with only a few visitors due to its location. Annually temple holds a Gozan Fire Festival – 5 different Kyoto Mountains have massive Japanese characters, and 5 different temples are responsible for mountains to alight.

Shrines

Yuki-jinja

This shrine was founded the same year as old Kyoto was founded. It has massive 800 years old trees and ancient stone lanterns. The shrine was built as a guardian of Kyoto. More information: https://kyoto.travel/en/shrine_temple/148.

Kitano-tenmangu

This shrine is dedicated to notable scholar and poet Tenjin. The shrine is famous for its numerous plum trees that were extremely loved by the scholar. Every year shrine holds a plum tree blossoming festival. More information: https://kyoto.travel/en/shrine_temple/142.

Kifune-jinja

It is a complex of three shrines and is over 1600 years old that makes it older than Kyoto itself. Shrine worships the God of rain and water. More information: https://kyoto.travel/en/shrine_temple/141.

Map of North Kyoto Temples and Shrines

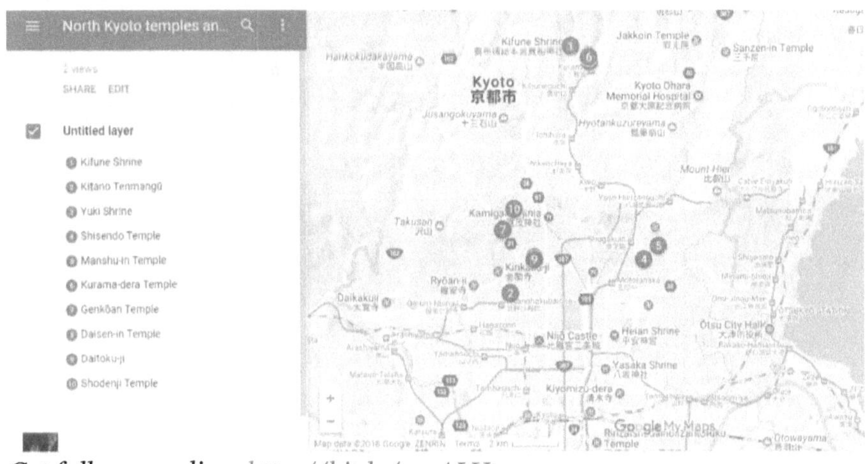

Get full map online: http://bit.ly/2zeALVt

East Kyoto Temples and Shrines

East Kyoto temples and shrines are mostly in the area of Higashiyama, so it's very easily reachable from any part of Kyoto.

Temples

Chion-in

This is an enormous and famous temple as most of Higashiyama walking tours include it in their trail. The temple was founded by Jodo (Pure Land) sect of Buddhism and is the head temple of this sect. Information: https://kyoto.travel/en/shrine_temple/151.

Main gates of Chion-in Temple

Eikan-do

Temple was founded in 853 by Esoteric Buddhism sect Shingon. It is very well-known for its autumn colors. More information: https://kyoto.travel/en/shrine_temple/152.

Hokan-ji

The temple is more known as Yasaka Pagoda that is 46 meters in height and standing in between of Kiyomizu-dera temple and Yasaka-Jinja Shrine. Tourists love it becomes its standing in the middle of old Kyoto street. More information: https://kyoto.travel/en/shrine_temple/155.

Kodai-ji

This temple is a very simple temple with beautiful architecture mostly from bamboo. It has two tea houses that are well known between locals. More about temple itself here: https://kyoto.travel/en/shrine_temple/157.

Nanzen-ji

Head temple of Rinzai sect of Zen Buddhism. This temple is one of the grandest temples in a whole Kyoto and surrounding areas. It has a massive front gate and beautiful gardens that will let your mind to rest. If you want to know more about this beautiful temple, follow this link: https://kyoto.travel/en/shrine_temple/158.

Aqueduct in Nanzen-ji Temple

Sanjusangen-do

Temple name can be translated as 'Hall with thirty-three spaces between the columns' that refers to the 120 meters long wooden building. There are 28 statues of deities that guard temple and is suitable for people who adore Japanese art. More information: https://kyoto.travel/en/shrine_temple/159.

Shoren-in

This temple has four famous gardens that are very popular with visitors coming from Higashiyama streets. More information about the temple is here: https://kyoto.travel/en/shrine_temple/160.

Kennin-ji

The temple is incredibly famous for various types of Chinese tea, so make sure you visit this one for an afternoon tea. Information: https://kyoto.travel/en/shrine_temple/255.

Shrines

Yasaka-jinja

Shrine was founded in 876 and is closely connected to Kyoto Geiko (Geisha) community. It's relatively small and colorful shrine that holds various festivals. More information: https://kyoto.travel/en/shrine_temple/161.

Heian-Jingu

Very colorful and bright shrine, built in 1895 so it's pretty new. It has a lovely garden filled with blossoming flowers and trees. Information about the shrine: https://kyoto.travel/en/shrine_temple/154.

Map of East Kyoto Temples and Shrines

Get the map: <http://bit.ly/2uaDoU7>

West Kyoto Temples and Shrines

West Kyoto is mostly Arashiyama district that is quite far from the central area of Kyoto. There are only some spectacular temples, but no shrines.

Temples

Daikaku-ji

Temple was once an Imperial Villa and now is the temple of treasures – beautiful Japanese art relics are stored in the temple and are available to visitors' eyes. More information about the temple's history: https://kyoto.travel/en/shrine_temple/163.

Gio-ji

Temple is surrounded by thick forest and always lies in the deep shade. Inside temple's main building there is a statue of Dainichi Nyorai (Buddha of Light). Temple is very famous for its autumn colors. More information: https://kyoto.travel/en/shrine_temple/164.

Gio-ji and its garden in the autumn

Koryu-ji

The temple was founded in 603 and is the oldest temple in Kyoto. It's a tiny temple and a perfect place to relax your body and mind. More information: https://kyoto.travel/en/shrine_temple/166.

Taizo-in

This temple can be described as a heart of Japanese Zen Buddhism and is very famous for its tea ceremonies and perfect Zen cuisine. Definitively worth visiting. More information: https://kyoto.travel/en/shrine_temple/169.

Map of West Kyoto Temples

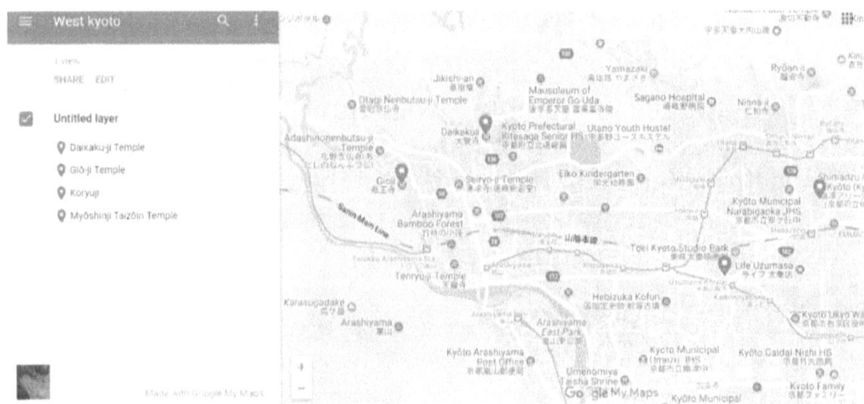

Get map: http://bit.ly/2tUPNuD

South Kyoto Temples and Shrines

South Kyoto most famous temples and shrines are located just 20-30 minutes from the city center, so it's effortless to visit them when you don't have much time in Kyoto.

Temples

Sennyu-ji
This temple is located at the foot of mountain Tsukinowa in Southern Higashiyama district. Temple has a mausoleum and serves as the mourning temple for the Imperial family. More information you will find here: https://kyoto.travel/en/shrine_temple/181.

Tofuku-ji
Tofuku-ji temple is one of five mountain temples of Rinzai Zen Buddhism. Temple is well known for its autumn foliage and gets lots of visitors during that time. Also, it has a 22 meters high *sanmon* gate that is the oldest gate of Zen Buddhism temples. If you are interested in the temple's history, you can find out more here: https://kyoto.travel/en/shrine_temple/182.

Wonderful wooden building of Tofuku-ji temple

Shrines

Fushimi Inari-Taisha

Famous Fushimi Inari's torii gate and two girls wearing kimono

Shrine belongs to the Hata clan and worships the god of rice and *sake*. The most famous part of the shrine is the steady path of 5000 orange colored *torii* gates. Also, the shrine has numerous statues of stone foxes. Everyone agrees that Fushimi Inari shrine is the most famous shrine in the whole of Japan. More information: https://kyoto.travel/en/shrine_temple/180.

Map of South Kyoto Temples and Shrines

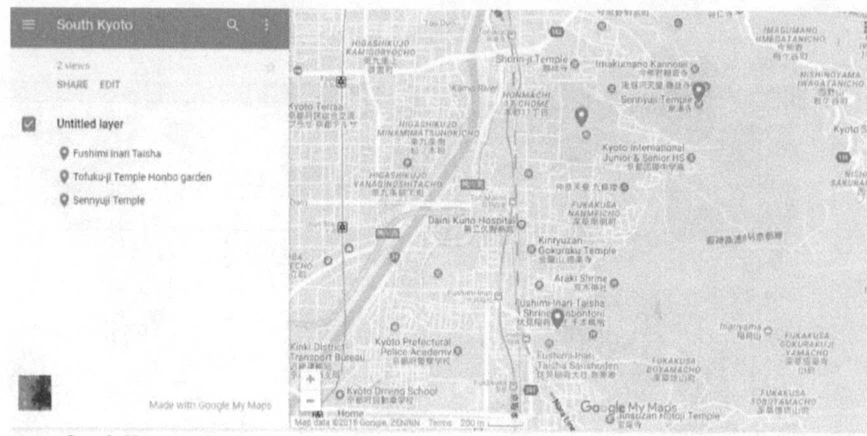

Get the full map here: http://bit.ly/2Nu2cOh

1st Day in Kyoto: Higashiyama/Gion, Downtown, and Fushimi Inari Shrine

8 AM. Arrival at the hotel. Always take the morning flight or train so you can have enough time for sightseeing. If there is no possibility to take morning flight/train, get an extra day for late evening arrival and check in the hotel.

8:30 AM. Breakfast. If your accommodation provides breakfast, eat breakfast and get ready to go out. If you have to buy breakfast, try to get out of the hotel and find the nearest coffee shop for the quick breakfast.

9 AM. Kiyomizu-dera Temple. If you are staying in our recommended Kyoto Garden Ryokan Yachiyo, go to bus stop Higashiyamaniomon bus stop (walk time ~10 min) and take a bus to Gojozaka (travel time ~8 min). Gojozaka bus stop is in front of the main entrance of Kiyomizu-dera temple. If you are staying somewhere else or don't want to use the bus, get a taxi to Gojo-Kawaramachi intersection. Walk Gojo-zaka street up the hill or just follow other people, you will need to turn to Chawan-zaka street that isolates you from all sorts of cities' noises. Enter the temple and explore it. Follow this link if you want to find out more about the temple and useful information: https://www.insidekyoto.com/kiyomizu-dera-temple.

Kiyomizu-dera gate during cherry blossom season

10:10 AM. Sannen-zaka and Ninen-zaka streets. Find the front of temple and exit via it, walk down Matsubara-Dori street – very easy to notice as it is lined with various gift shops. After following the street, you will reach another very well preserved and lined with wooden houses street – Sannen-zaka street. Then Sannen-zaka flattens a little bit, turn slightly right and you will reach another traditional street called Ninen-zaka. These streets represent the old Kyoto and are filled with traditional teahouses, restaurants, and shops. You will see the most famous teashop Kasagiya, pop in and get a refreshing drink or ice cream to take away.
10:20 AM. Ishibei-koji street and Kodai-ji temple. Keep following Ninen-zaka street until you will see signs for Kodai-ji temple. Follow signs to the temple and turn to Ishibei-koji street just before the temple parking lot. This street is regarded as the most beautiful street in Japan. Just a few minutes away from Ishibei-koji street lies temple Kodai-ji. Relatively small and simple yet adorable.

Kodai-ji temple in the evening

10:55 AM. Maruyama-Koen Park. Follow the street to the north, and you will see a Maruyama-Koen Park – small park with beautiful cherry trees, on the foot of Higashiyama mountain and the perfect spot for the picnic.

11 AM. Chion-in Temple. Exit the north side of the park, keep going north until you see the massive gate and steep steps. Go up the steps and you will enter the courtyard of Chion-in. There is a possibility that the main hall will be under construction, so take that in mind.

11:20 AM. Shoren-in Temple. Keep heading to the north and you will see signs for another great temple – Shoren-in. It's a very small Tendai Buddhism temple that is usually very quiet as most of the tourist groups miss it. Get yourself a traditional Japanese green tea, some sweets like *mochi* and enjoy the view of the garden.

12:05 PM. Travel to Downtown and lunchtime. Exit the temple and walk downhill to reach a Higashiyama station on the Tozai subway line. Travel to Kyoto Shiyakushomae station. We recommend to head to Nishiki Market and get your lunch at one of the small traditional Japanese restaurants. Nishiki Market sells fresh fish, vegetables, sweets, and tea. There are some places to get a take away like sashimi or sit in and have nice homely food at one of the restaurants. You can either sit in or get a takeaway.

Take away food court in Nishiki Market

13:25 PM. Pontocho Alley. This alley is great for dining and night out, however, it is quite an expensive place so we recommend just to walk around and look at luxury buildings. This place is also great for spotting a *geisha*.

13:55 PM. Keihan Line to Fushimi Inari Station. Go to Shijo-Dori street, walk east across Kamogawa River, downstairs into Keihan Gion-Shijo Station. Buy your ticket and take Keihan line south to Fushimi Inari Sation. Be careful, don't go into the limited express train as it doesn't stop at Fushimi Inari.

14:25 PM. Fushimi Inari Taisha Shrine. Walk out of the station, turn left and walk up the hill, cross train tracks. The walk is very well marked, so you will easily find a way to the shrine. You will cross one major street and will see the first shrine's red-orange gate.

Fushimi Inari Taisha Shrine is a very famous shrine between locals and foreigners. It is renowned for its neverending torii path that was donated by various companies/people to the shrine.

We highly recommend you to take a hike to the summit of mountain Inari that is 233 meters high. This hike is a circular

66

pilgrimage hike that lasts for 5 kilometers and takes about 3 hours. The full guide of hiking can be found here: https://www.insidekyoto.com/fushimi-inari-hike-kyoto. Remember you don't have to do the entire hike if you don't feel like you can manage to do it.

God Fox statue at Fushimi Inari Taisha shrine

17:40 PM. Keihan Main Line to Gion-Shijo Station. After a tiring hike gets yourself a quick snack and a drink at the convenience store near the station. Get into Keihan Main Line heading to Gion-Shijo Station. The ride takes about 7-8 minutes.

18:00 PM. Dinner at Omen Kodai-ji. After getting to Gion-Shijo Station walk for 15 minutes and reach the restaurant. You have to walk on Shijo-Dori Street and follow the signs for Kodai-ji or Kiyomizu-dera Temple. Basically, you are coming back to Southern Higashiyama/Gion district and walking almost the same route that you've walked in the morning.

Myodai Omen Kodai-ji is an *udon* place located in the middle of several temples. It offers high standard *udon* at very affordable prices, and the menu is foreigners friendly. *Omen-*style *udon* is vegetarian style *udon* (warm or cold) served with soy-based dipping broth and various types of local Kyoto vegetables that can be either boiled or pickled. All the ingredients come separately, and you can add what you like into your broth by yourself.

19:30 PM. Evening at Gion Shimbashi. We hope that after the dinner you still have the energy to explore more. Start your evening stroll from Shijo-Ohashi Bridge, at the end of bridge cross Kawabata-Dori and follow Kawabata-Dori for about 100 meters. You will see a tree-lined lane, follow that to the east, and you will find the Shimbashi area (known as Shirakawa). Be prepared for the crowds as it's a trendy street in Kyoto. It runs from Hanami-koji to Kawabata-Dori. Shimbashi is packed with expensive shops and restaurants, traditional Japanese inns and numerous hostess clubs. The evening is the best for this part of Gion so keep your eyes opened.

21:00 PM. Going to the accommodation. Get the taxi back to your accommodation as it will be the best and fastest option. However, you are welcomed to take the subway or bus depending on where you are staying. Grab a snack on your way and take a rest at the hotel.

Map of the 1ˢᵗ Day in Kyoto

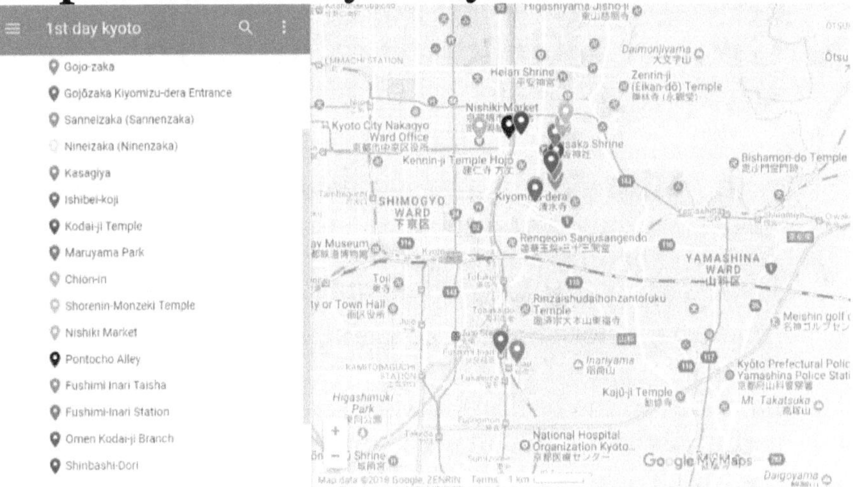

Get the full map here: *http://bit.ly/2KORp2x*

2nd Day in Kyoto: Arashiyama Including Tenryu-ji, Bamboo Groove, Kinkaku-ji and Hot Springs

7:30 AM. Wake up and get ready for breakfast. The earlier you start sightseeing, the most likely you are going to avoid the main tourist's crowds.

8:00 AM. Breakfast. Get a full breakfast at the hotel and somewhere close to your accommodation.

8:30 AM. Head to Arashiyama. Arashiyama district is quite far, so the best option is to take a taxi from your accommodation. If you are keen on saving money and are staying in our recommended accommodation, you can get a bus from Okazaki Jinjazen bus stop to Arashiyama Tenryuji-mae. The journey time is 40 minutes.

9:15 AM. Tenryu-ji Temple. The original temple was built in 1339. However, the buildings you see now were established in 1900. It is surrounded by a beautiful 14th-century Zen garden. Make sure to check out the garden and inside the main hall.

10:20 AM. Arashiyama Bamboo Groove. Leave temple by the north gate that is located in the garden and take a left trail. The trail will lead you to the famous Arashiyama Bamboo Groove. This forest usually described as magical and breath-taking. Walk all the way uphill.

Path in Arashiyama Bamboo Groove

10:50 AM. Okochi-Sanso Villa. At the top of the hill, you will see a gorgeous villa that was home to a Japanese samurai actor. You will have to pay for the entrance 1000 yen ($9). It's a little bit expensive, but you will get a most unusual Japanese tree and a cake after the garden tour. It's like killing two birds with the same stone.

Okochi-Sanso Villa

11:55 AM. Kameyama-Koen Park. Get out of the villa and head to the main street, and walk south – you will be almost returning to the Tenryu-ji temple. This time head more to the riverside and you will see signs directing to Kameyama-Koen Park (Arashiyama Park Kameyama Area). The park is locally famous for the monkeys which if you are lucky, you will be able to see them. Go to the hilltop and enjoy a spectacular view of the river.

12:40 PM. Lunch at Yudofu Sagano. Exit by the south exit of Kameyama-Koen Park, pass the public toilets and follow the Katsura River, then head to the direction of another public toilet, head straight till you see a hotel called Ranzan. The restaurant Yudofu Sagano is going to be in front of the hotel.

Yudofu Sagano specializes in Arashiyama's Buddhist specialty – *yudo* (chunks of tofu simmered in the broth). This dish is called Arashiyama's specialty as initially, Arashiyama was a district filled with temples and monks that demanded the vegetarian food. That's how *yudo* became very famous. *Yudo* is always served with various types of side dishes.

14:00 PM. Head to Ninna-ji temple. Walk to Arashiyama Tenryuji-mae stop and take the bus to Sigatoka bus stop. It will take about 13 minutes. Get off at Sigatoka bus stop and walk north, follow signs for Ninna-ji temple.

14:35 PM. Ninna-ji Temple. This temple is included in UNESCO World Heritage list. Ninna-ji was initially built in 888, but most of the buildings you see now were established in 1600. The temple has a beautiful garden with lots of ponds, cherry trees, and flowers.

15:30 PM. Head to Kinkaku-ji Temple. Exit by the south gate and find an Omuroninnaji bus stop, take the bus and get off at Kinkakujimae bus stop. Journey time is 7 minutes by bus and 10 minutes by walk.

15:55 PM. Kinkaku-ji Temple. This temple is usually referred as a Golden Pavilion as its two floors are covered in gold. Kinkaku-ji is not only famous for its golden roof but also for a beautiful garden with a pond that surrounds the temple. Relax your tired legs here and enjoy the beauty of this temple. Don't forget to take some photos!

Kinkaku-ji Golden Pavilion

17:00 PM. Kinkaku Soft Ice Cream. Get out of the temple, pass through the parking lot and keep going straight till you find street vendors of souvenirs and food. You will see a little vendor kiosk saying 'Kinkaku Soft' – that's a green tea and red beans soft ice cream. The ice cream is famous because its top layer is golden representing Kinkaku-ji temple's roof and cone represents its base floor. It is said that this ice cream is the most delicious ice cream in Kyoto.

17:30 PM. Head to Tenzan-no-yu Onsen. Kinkaku-ji temple has a really inconvenient line and stops for the public transportation. Take a taxi to Tenzan-no-yu Onsen. It will take about 20 minutes to get to your destination.

17:55 PM. Tenzan-no-yu Onsen (Hot Springs). Locals say that is the best hot springs in the whole Kyoto and we believe the same. Outdoor *Onsen* (hot springs) are natural and coming from the well drilled 1200 meters below Kyoto. Inside hot springs uses just regular water, so you definitely have to go to the outdoor ones. Also, real *Onsen* water is suitable for various health issues and helps your body to relax faster. We highly recommend trying any of suggested massages for an extra price.

19:50 PM. Dinner. You might be starving from a tiring day and spending so much time in Onsen. Luckily, you don't need to go somewhere else as Tenzan-no-yu Onsen has an excellent restaurant that is incredibly famous for its traditional Kyoto food. Enjoy your meal.

21:00 PM. An evening walk by Katsura River. Leave Tenzan-no-yu Onsen and head to the river direction – takes up to 10 minutes. Enjoy a short walk along the river with beautiful scenery.

Katsura River at night

21:40 PM. Head back to your accommodation. We suggest taking a taxi as it will be hard to catch any public transportation and it will take too long to get home and rest.

Map of the 2nd Day in Kyoto

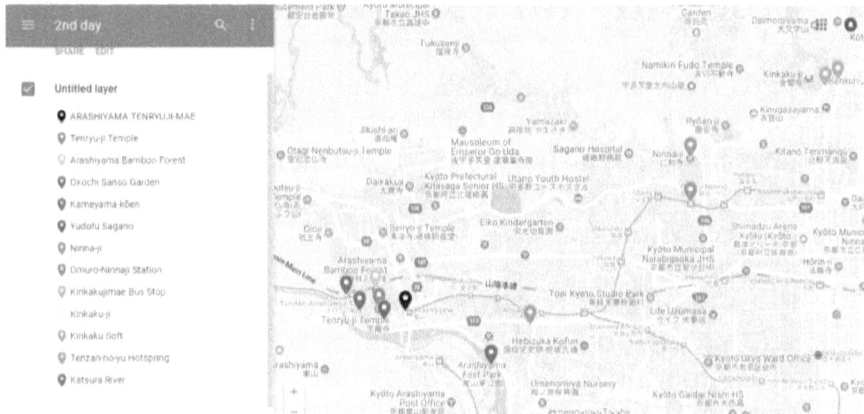

Get a full map online: http://bit.ly/2moXLoT

3rd Day in Kyoto: Northern Higashiyama and Leaving Kyoto

7:30 AM. Get Ready. Pack your luggage before breakfast and ask the receptionist if you could arrange a luggage delivery to the airport, bus or train station. Most likely you will be able to send your luggage for a small price.

8:00 AM. Breakfast. Get breakfast that fills you up till afternoon.

8:30 AM. Taxi to Ginkaku-ji temple. From accommodation get a taxi to Ginkaku-ji temple that is located in Northern Higashiyama. Depending on where you are staying, the journey time shouldn't take more than 30 minutes.

9:00 AM. Ginkaku-ji Temple. The temple is located at the base of Higashiyama Mountains. Ginkaku-ji temple is also closed 'Silver Pavilion' and is a sister temple of Kinkaku-ji temple. It is a really spectacular temple, so take your time to explore it.

Ginkaku-ji temple and the pond

10:00 AM. Path of Philosophy. Exit the temple and walk down the hill for about 100 meters. You will end up walking a famous 'Path of Philosophy' (*Tetsugaku-no-Michi*) that is a path along the canal from Ginkaku-ji temple to Nanzen-ji.

Take your time to enjoy the beautiful view of nature and a relaxing walk. You will find several tea and coffee stalls, so get yourself a drink.

11:15 AM. Nanzen-ji Temple. At the end of the path, you will see another famous Kyoto's temple. There are two beautiful garden sections: inner and outer. The outside garden is open 24/7, and the inner garden is only accessible when the temple is open. Enter the temple and enjoy beautiful, relaxing Zen gardens and great architecture of the temple. You will definitely need a couple of hours to see everything.

Simple wooden Nanzen-ji temple's hall and gardens in the background

13:00 PM. Lunch at Hinode-Udon. Just 10 minutes of walk from Nanzen-ji temple – you have to get out of the temple and head north like you coming back to the 'Path of Philosophy.' You will easily spot Hinode-Udon restaurant that sells the best curry udon – udon noodles with curry sauce. You can select the spiciness level and enjoy unusual combination between udon and curry – something that you will never find somewhere else.

14:00 PM. Souvenirs. Around temples and 'Path of Philosophy' various street vendors sell great souvenirs related to Kyoto. We would recommend you to buy things related to the temples as it represents Kyoto the best. You could buy souvenirs such as bracelets, keyrings, little statues and fridge magnets – they are light and easy to transport. **15:00 PM. Head to airport/bus or train station.** Find the closest train or bus stop, or you can take a taxi to the place from where you are departing. If you are flying, try to get an early evening flight as you will have enough time to visit last temples and to travel to the airport.

Map of 3rd Day in Kyoto

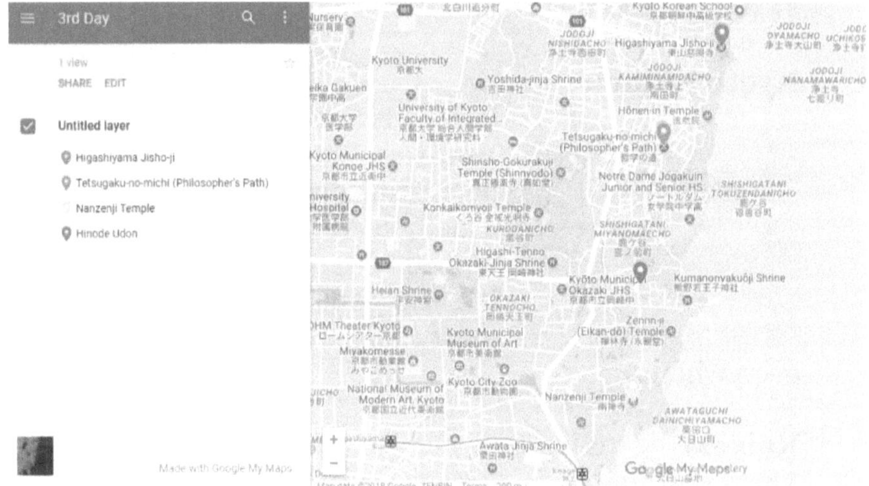

Get the full map here: *http://bit.ly/2JcFJ4O*

Guide to Kyoto's Food: How to Eat like a Local?

Kyoto Ramen

Ramen is famous in all Japan. However, Ramen is different depending on the area. Kyoto ramen is usually served with pork broth and topped with pork and some vegetables. It's very popular with students as it's quite cheap and there are restaurants everywhere.

Kaiseki

Kaiseki is a high-end multi-course that includes various dishes served in small plates and bowls. There are two kinds of kaiseki: tea kaiseki and formal kaiseki. Tae Kaiseki is served together with a tea and is a light meal, while formal kaiseki includes a full course of food – can consist of from 50 to 80 different little dishes!

Shojin Ryori

Shojin Ryori is Zen temple vegetarian cuisine. It came from China in the 13th century. The meal consists of various vegetables, soups, and rice. It is considered as very healthy and filling meal, and inexpensive. You can find multiple restaurants serving *shojin ryori* near temples.

Yuba

Yuba is basically a tofu skin that is made from soybean as tofu is. Yuba is very famous in Kyoto, and various restaurants sell great yuba with broth and some vegetables. Locals say that Kyoto is the best place to taste real Japanese yuba.

Matcha Desserts

Japanese green tea is commonly known as matcha, and there are various types of desserts that are made from matcha such as donuts, ice cream, cakes and etc. You can find matcha desserts everywhere around Kyoto, and they are usually even cheaper than western desserts.

Kyo Wagashi

Wagashi is a traditional Japanese sweet, so Kyo Wagashi is Kyoto traditional Japanese sweets. Sweet are usually very colorful and filled with red bean paste. Kyo sweets are typically served with matcha at the traditional tea house.

Yudofu

Yudofu is a specialty in Kyoto. Yudofu is hot tofu served in a beef/pork/vegetable broth. It's a simple but delicious meal that can be found easily anywhere in Kyoto.

Okonomiyaki

It's just a savory pancake with various toppings such as chopped cabbage, other vegetables, sauce and sometimes seafood. Kyoto is famous for its okonomiyaki as restaurants, or market stalls make them extra-large.

Mackerel Soba

A local delicacy in Kyoto – sweet stewed mackerel at the top of soba is one of the most popular dishes in Kyoto. Soba is buckwheat noodles that gives a little bit of savory taste that is a perfect combination with sweet mackerel taste.

Thank you

Thank you for choosing this travel guide for your fantastic journey to Kyoto. We hope that this guide will help you to plan your trip and make the best of it, and you will enjoy all our planned activities. You are very welcome to leave your feedback, just need to send an email to admin@guidora.com. Wish you a pleasant and adventurous trip.

Your friends at Guidora